Rookie
Read-About® Geography

North Dakota

By Pam Zollman

Consultants

Reading Adviser
Nanci R. Vargus, EdD
Assistant Professor of Literacy
University of Indianapolis, Indianapolis, Indiana

Subject Adviser
Charles Pace
Director
Fargo Public Library
Fargo, North Dakota

Children's Press®
A Division of Scholastic Inc.
New York   Toronto   London   Auckland   Sydney
Mexico City   New Delhi   Hong Kong
Danbury, Connecticut

Designer: Herman Adler Design
Photo Researcher: Caroline Anderson
The photo on the cover shows buffalo grazing in Theodore Roosevelt
National Park, North Dakota.

Library of Congress Cataloging-in-Publication Data

Zollman, Pam.
   North Dakota / by Pam Zollman.
      p. cm. — (Rookie read–about geography)
   Includes index.
   ISBN 0-516-25259-3 (lib. bdg.)   0-516-25159-7 (pbk.)
 1. North Dakota—Juvenile literature. 2. North Dakota—Geography—
Juvenile literature. I. Title. II. Series.
   F636.3.Z65 2005
   917.84'02—dc22   2005002142

CHILDREN'S PRESS, and ROOKIE READ-ABOUT®,
and associated logos are trademarks and/or registered trademarks
of Scholastic Library Publishing. SCHOLASTIC and associated logos
are trademarks and/or registered trademarks of Scholastic Inc.

1 2 3 4 5 6 7 8 9 10 R 14 13 12 11 10 09 08 07 06 05

Which state is called the
Peace Garden State?

It is North Dakota!

North Dakota is shaped like a rectangle.

Can you find North Dakota on this map?

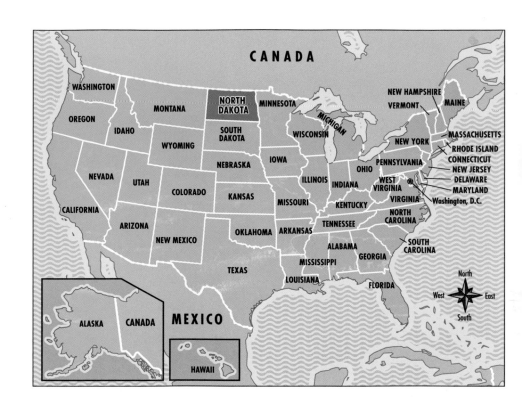

CANADA

WASHINGTON

OREGON

IDAHO

MONTANA

NORTH DAKOTA

MINNESOTA

NEW HAMPSHIRE

VERMONT

MAINE

WYOMING

SOUTH DAKOTA

WISCONSIN

MICHIGAN

NEW YORK

MASSACHUSETTS

RHODE ISLAND

CONNECTICUT

NEVADA

UTAH

COLORADO

NEBRASKA

IOWA

ILLINOIS

INDIANA

OHIO

PENNSYLVANIA

WEST VIRGINIA

NEW JERSEY

DELAWARE

MARYLAND

CALIFORNIA

ARIZONA

NEW MEXICO

KANSAS

MISSOURI

KENTUCKY

VIRGINIA

Washington, D.C.

OKLAHOMA

ARKANSAS

TENNESSEE

NORTH CAROLINA

TEXAS

MISSISSIPPI

ALABAMA

GEORGIA

SOUTH CAROLINA

LOUISIANA

FLORIDA

ALASKA

CANADA

MEXICO

HAWAII

North

West

East

South

5

North Dakota touches Canada. Canada is the country to the north of the United States.

The International Peace Garden spans the border between Canada and the United States.

In this garden, a person can stand in both nations at the same time!

North Dakota has three regions.

They are the Red River Valley, the Drift Prairie, and the Great Plains.

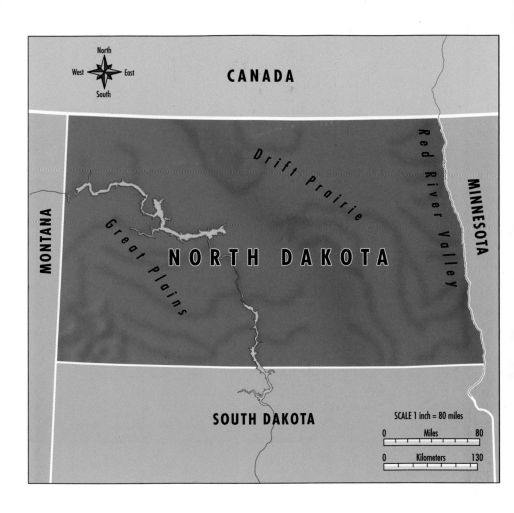

CANADA

North
West — East
South

Drift Prairie

Red River Valley

MINNESOTA

MONTANA

Great Plains

NORTH DAKOTA

SOUTH DAKOTA

SCALE 1 inch = 80 miles

| 0 | Miles | 80 |

| 0 | Kilometers | 130 |

The Red River Valley is
flat. It is good for farming.

Farmers grow wheat, beans, sugar beets, barley, and sunflowers.

The Drift Prairie has streams, lakes, and rolling hills.

Devils Lake is North Dakota's largest natural lake. Some people like to fish there.

13

14

The Great Plains cover
half of North Dakota. It is
a good place to raise cattle.

North Dakota has many
ranches.

A part of the Great
Plains Region is called the
Badlands. Early explorers
named this area.

The Badlands has rocks in
strange shapes.

This is the capitol in Bismarck, North Dakota.

Bismarck is North Dakota's state capital.

Fargo is North Dakota's largest city. People in Fargo make computer software, concrete, and metal parts.

Jamestown is halfway
between Bismarck
and Fargo.

The largest buffalo
statue in the world is
in Jamestown.

North Dakota has antelope, moose, deer, and bighorn sheep.

These are bighorn sheep.

The state bird is the
western meadowlark.

These are wild turkeys.

Wild turkeys, Canada geese, and grouse live in North Dakota, too.

North Dakota's rivers have catfish, trout, and pike.

Winters in North Dakota
are long and very cold.
People like to go sledding,
skating, and ice fishing in
the winter.

Summers can be hot.
People like to swim, golf,
ride horses, and hike in
the summer.

27

28

What would you like to do in North Dakota?

Words You Know

Badlands

bighorn sheep

Bismarck

buffalo

Devils Lake

International Peace
Garden

sunflowers

western meadowlark

Index

About the Author

Pam Zollman is an award-winning author of short stories and books for children.
She was born in Texas and lived most of her life there. Now she lives in the
Pocono Mountains of Pennsylvania.

Photo Credits

Photographs © 2005: Bruce Coleman Inc./Joy Spurr: 3; Corbis Images: 23, 31
bottom right (Darrell Gulin), 14 (Richard Hamilton Smith); Dembinsky Photo
Assoc.: 17, 24, 30 top left (Dominique Braud), 22, 30 top right (Doug Locke);
PhotoEdit: 18, 30 bottom left (Dennis MacDonald), 28 (Barbara Stitzer); The
Image Works/Jenny Hager: cover; The International Peace Garden: 6, 31 top
right; Tom Bean: 10, 11, 13, 21, 27, 30 bottom right, 31 bottom left, 31 top left.
Maps by Bob Italiano